Merry Bot Christmas

Tame Holiday Stress with Your Santa Bot

Sugar Gay Isber McMillan

The WOW Book Co.™

Austin, Texas

Published by
The WOW Book Co.™
Austin, Texas, USA

Book design by The WOW Book Co.™
Logo and QR codes included with permission.

Large Font Edition / Talk to Your Tools™

Printed in the United States of America

ISBN: 978-1-967973-50-7

Table of Contents

Chapter 1. Why Holidays Feel Hard
Chapter 2. Your Bot as a Holiday Helper
Chapter 3. Food, Family, and Finding Balance
Chapter 4. Gift Ideas with a Little Help
Chapter 5. Decorations, Traditions, and Memories
Chapter 6. Handling Travel Stress
Chapter 7. Conversations Made Easier
Chapter 8. Finding Calm with Prompts
Chapter 9. Gratitude, Prayer, and Journaling
Chapter 10. Sleep, Rest, and Renewal
Chapter 11. Crisis Helper
Chapter 12. Chatting with Your Bot When You're Stressed

Appendix: Printables & Templates
About the Author
A Final Word

Introduction

Picture the holidays at the North Pole. Santa sits in his chair with a long list. The sleigh is waiting. The elves are busy - wrapping, packing, checking twice. Every toy is measured, every bow is tied, every stocking is filled. Santa may be the one who delivers the gifts, but it is the elves who make the magic happen.

That is how ChatGPT works for you. You are Santa. You know the wishes, the family traditions, the problems to solve. ChatGPT is your elf, working quietly in the background, taking your requests and turning them into answers, lists, and ideas that make the season brighter.

Now, if you have never used ChatGPT before, here is the first thing you need to know: it is not Google. You do not just type in a question and get a page of links.

ChatGPT is a conversation partner. You tell it what you need, and it answers in full sentences as if you were speaking to a friend.

It is easy to use on a phone, but most people find it works best on a computer. On a bigger screen, you can see the conversation unfold, scroll back to review, and copy prompts or results without losing your place.

Before you start, imagine you are giving your elf some instructions. You can say:

- "I need help with holiday planning."
- "Answer like you are an expert in Christmas shopping."
- "Write as if you are Santa's best helper."

ChatGPT will take that direction and play the role you assign. It is like ringing the sleigh bells and watching the elves spring into action.

This book will show you how to put your new elf to work.

Inside, you will find ways to save money, save time, and add magic back into the season. There will be prompts you can copy word for word, tips to try in your own voice, and plenty of holiday cheer to keep the stress away.

Think of it this way: with ChatGPT at your side, you never face the season alone. Your elf is always ready. The lists get shorter, the ideas get better, and the holidays feel lighter. That is the promise.

ChatGPT can:

- Plan menus and grocery lists

- Suggest gifts for every age and budget
- Write holiday letters, cards or invitations
- Come up with games and trivia for a family gathering
- Help you find deals or stretch your holiday budget

Other chatbots exist but most are built for a single job. One may help with shopping, another with your calendar. ChatGPT is flexible. It can do all of these tasks and more. It is like having your own Santa Bot ready to pitch in whenever you need it.

The Promise: Save Money, Save Time, Add Magic

This book is full of ready-to-use prompts and examples. Each one is designed to save you money, save you time and add more magic to the season.

- Save Money: Find coupons, bundle deals and creative ways to give without overspending.
- Save Time: Create a meal plan, a gift list or a party invitation in minutes.
- Add Magic: Ask ChatGPT to spin a bedtime story, invent a scavenger hunt or write a toast for your holiday dinner.

You do not need to be tech-savvy to make it work. The prompts are simple. The results will surprise you. With a little help from your Santa Bot, the holidays can feel less like a chore and more like the joyful celebration they are meant to be.

Sample Prompts

- *"Write a 3-day grocery list for Christmas dinner for 8 people under $100."*
- *"Suggest 5 thoughtful Secret Santa gifts under $15 for a coworker who loves coffee."*
- *"Create a fun holiday trivia game for a family gathering with kids and grandparents."*
- *"Write a heartfelt thank-you note to my boss after the holiday party."*
- *"Give me 3 ways to decorate my small apartment for under $30."*

Why the Holidays Feel Overwhelming

Every year, the season sneaks up on us. The calendar fills with school concerts, office parties and family gatherings. The to-do list grows longer every time you look at it. You still have to shop for gifts, cook meals, clean the house and travel across town or across the country.

Budgets are stretched thin. Ads shout about sales you cannot miss. Social media scrolls past with perfect trees, picture-perfect dinners and families in matching pajamas. It all looks wonderful but it can leave you feeling tired before the fun even begins.

You are not alone. Almost everyone feels a mix of joy and stress this time of year.

The good news is that there is a way to make the season easier, calmer and even more magical.

Why the Holidays Feel Overwhelming

- Too many events packed into too little time
- Budget pressure from gifts, travel, and food
- Family expectations and traditions colliding with reality
- Work deadlines that don't pause for December
- The constant noise - ads, sales, "perfect" holiday images on social media

How ChatGPT Can Be Your Secret Helper

Think of it this way. With ChatGPT at your side, you're no longer facing the holidays alone. Instead of juggling tasks until you drop, you'll have a clever helper ready to guide you, answer questions, and smooth out the rough edges of the season.

Why do the holidays feel overwhelming? Because it isn't just one thing. It's the long lists that never end. It's the gift shopping you put off until the last minute. It's the pressure to cook the perfect meal and decorate the house like it came out of a magazine.

It's the travel, the weather, the family dynamics, and the feeling that there's never enough time. All of it lands at once, and no wonder so many people dread what should be the happiest season of the year.

Here's the good news. You don't have to do this the hard way anymore. ChatGPT can be the extra set of hands you've always wished for.

Think of it as your own holiday elf, working behind the scenes while you take the credit. You'll learn how to get instant gift ideas that actually fit the person, draft cheerful holiday letters in minutes, plan meals without breaking your budget, and even come up with fun new traditions to make your family laugh.

And here's something else: these tips don't stop on December 25th. The same tools you use to survive Christmas shopping can help you plan New Year's Eve parties, write your resolutions, and even start the year with less stress and more clarity. The gift of this book is that it doesn't just prepare you for one holiday - it prepares you for many.

So, here's my promise to you. If you keep reading, you'll discover shortcuts, scripts, and strategies that will save time, save money, and bring more joy back into the season.

No more all-nighters wrapping gifts, no more grocery store panic, no more staring at a blank card with nothing to say. This is your chance to reclaim the holidays, to laugh more, and to enjoy what matters.

Your next holiday can be one you remember with a smile. Let's get started.

Think of it this way: You are Santa Claus. You want everything ready for the big holiday. The meals. The gifts. The magic. But even Santa can't do it all alone. He has elves at the North Pole, working day and night.

ChatGPT is your elf.

Always ready. Always cheerful. Always quick.

Before we dive into the fun, let's get practical. The holidays are wonderful, but they can also drain your wallet faster than a toy store on Christmas Eve. Travel, groceries, gifts, decorations, it all adds up.

This is where your Santa Bot can shine the brightest. Imagine having a little helper who remembers every coupon, spots the best deals, and helps you stretch your budget without cutting the joy. That's the kind of magic we're starting with.

So pour yourself a mug of cocoa, take a deep breath,

And let's open the workshop doors.

Chapter 1: Save Money with ChatGPT

The jingling of sleigh bells is wonderful, but the sound of your bank account groaning? Not so festive.

Every year, families feel the pinch: plane tickets jump in price, grocery lists grow longer, and the perfect gifts somehow always seem just a little too expensive.

But here's the good news: your Santa Bot is here to help. Think of ChatGPT as an elf who knows every shortcut in the workshop.

You don't have to scroll through ten websites hunting for deals or wonder if there's a coupon floating around out there. You ask, it answers. Fast, friendly, and ready to keep your holiday bright without breaking the bank.

Finding Cheaper Tickets (Travel & Events)

Holiday travel is one of the biggest budget busters. Flights and hotels climb higher than the star on the tree. But you can use ChatGPT to:

Generate lists of budget airlines or discount travel sites

Ask for alternative airports near your destination

Find the cheapest travel dates for your route

Compare hotel vs. Airbnb options in seconds

Prompt example:
"**Find the cheapest flight options from Dallas to New York in December, including nearby airports and travel date suggestions to save money**."

Gift Hacks: Buy-One-Get-One, Bundles, Coupons

Santa knows how to get a deal — and now so can you. Ask ChatGPT to:

- Search for bundle deals (like a board game set instead of buying pieces separately)
- Suggest buy-one-get-one holiday offers
- Pull together coupon codes or discount sites to try
- Recommend DIY gift bundles (like movie night baskets or hot cocoa kits) that cost less but look luxe

Prompt example:
"Suggest ten budget-friendly DIY gift bundles under $25 that look expensive but are easy to put together."

Grocery Budget Planning

Holiday feasts are joyful, but grocery bills can snowball. With ChatGPT you can:

- Turn recipes into shopping lists with exact amounts
- Plan budget-friendly menus that reuse ingredients
- Ask for substitutions (swap out pricey nuts for affordable seeds, or fancy cuts of meat for crowd-pleasing roasts)
- Get ideas for make-ahead meals that save both money and stress

Prompt example:

"Make a holiday dinner menu for six people under $75 using affordable grocery store ingredients."

Comparison Shopping Made Simple

No more wandering the digital aisles, checking every site one by one. ChatGPT can:

Compare toys, gadgets, or clothes side by side

Suggest reliable lower-cost alternatives to pricey gifts

Help you decide when to buy now vs. wait for a sale

Point out which stores offer free shipping or extended returns

Prompt example:
"Compare three popular wireless headphones under $100 with pros, cons and best holiday deals."

Why ChatGPT, Not Just Google?

Google will throw a hundred links your way. ChatGPT gives you one clear answer, written like a helpful friend. You don't waste time clicking around. Instead, you get suggestions shaped to your exact budget, family size, or special requests. That's the difference between searching and having a Santa's helper whispering in your ear.

Wrapping It Up

Saving money doesn't mean cutting the magic. With a few smart prompts, you can keep your wallet jolly and still deliver sparkling gifts,

feasts, and travel plans. ChatGPT turns hours of hunting into minutes of planning. That means more time for cocoa, carols, and memory-making.

And speaking of magic, now that your budget is safe and sound, let's talk about the most joyful part of all: finding the perfect gifts.

How to Talk to Your Chatbot (And Get the Best Results)

Think of your chatbot as a friendly helper sitting across the kitchen table, waiting to make your life easier. The more details you give, the better the answers. If you only say "Give me gift ideas," you might get something too general. But if you paint a picture — age, hobbies, price range — you'll get answers that feel almost handpicked.

Example 1: Gift Shopping

Instead of typing:

"Gift ideas for a boy"

Try this:

"Frankie is 6 years old. He loves baseball and dinosaurs. Show me 10 gift ideas under $50 that would make him smile."

Result: A list of toys, games, books, and activities that match Frankie's real interests and your budget.

Example 2: Grocery Savings

Instead of typing:

"Cheap meals"

Try this:

Plan 5 dinner ideas for a family of four that cost under $15 each. Please include a shopping list and keep prep time under 30 minutes.

Result: A week's worth of meals plus a ready-to-go list for the store.

Example 3: Holiday Letters

Instead of typing:

"Write a Christmas letter"

Try this:

Write a one-page holiday letter from a family with three kids, ages 4, 8, and 11. Mention that the youngest learned to ride a bike, the middle child starred in the school play, and the oldest just started middle school. Keep it funny and warm."

Result: A letter you can personalize and send without hours of struggle.

Example 4: Stress Busters

Instead of typing:

"Help me relax"

Try this:

"Give me 5 quick stress-busting tips I can do in under 10 minutes while the cookies are in the oven. Keep it lighthearted and holiday themed.

Result: Instant relief in the middle of holiday chaos.

The secret is this: give your chatbot the same details you'd give a helpful friend. Who, what, when, where and budget. Add a touch of your personality and you'll get answers that feel like magic.

Holiday Starter Kit: Prompts You Can Copy Today

Try these to see how quickly your Santa Bot can help you:

- **Gift Ideas**

"Give me 10 gift ideas for a 12-year-old who loves art and animals. Keep each under $30."

- **Stocking Stuffers**

"Suggest 15 fun stocking stuffers under $10 for teenagers that are not candy."

- **Holiday Letter**

"Write a warm and funny one-page Christmas letter for a couple with two dogs who just moved into a new house."

- **Meal Planning**

"Plan a holiday dinner for 6 people with turkey, two sides, and a dessert. Keep the grocery list under $75."

- **Travel Prep**

"Make a packing list for a family of 4 going to Colorado for 5 days in December. Include clothes, toiletries, and fun extras."

- **Party Fun**

"Create 10 icebreaker questions for a holiday office party that are family friendly and fun."

- **DIY Decor**

"Give me 5 simple DIY holiday centerpiece ideas using candles, fruit, or pinecones."

- **Stress Relief**

"List 7 quick ways to relax when holiday stress hits. Keep each one under 5 minutes."

Tip: *Always tell your chatbot the age, number of people, budget and theme. The more details you give, the more magical the answers.*

Chapter 2. The Perfect Gift Guide

The holidays are about giving, but sometimes finding the right gift feels harder than stringing lights on a twenty-foot tree. With ChatGPT as your holiday helper, you can skip the stress and unlock endless ideas.

Whether you are shopping on a tight budget, need something last-minute, or want to create a memory instead of wrapping another gadget, this chapter will show you how to turn prompts into perfect presents.

Last-Minute Gifts (Under $20, Printable, DIY)

We have all been there. A neighbor drops by with a plate of cookies and suddenly you need a gift to give back. ChatGPT can save you.

Example Prompt:
"List 15 last-minute holiday gifts under $20 that I can buy today or print at home."

Sample Results:

- Printable coupon for a coffee date
- A set of homemade spice mixes with recipe cards

- Digital puzzle or game app gift codes
- A festive holiday-scented candle
- DIY hot cocoa kit in a mason jar

DIY Twist:
Ask ChatGPT to generate simple instructions.
"Write easy steps for a homemade sugar scrub with ingredients I probably already have at home."

Why It Works: These quick solutions can be printed, cooked, or crafted in an hour. No panic, just joy.

Hook to keep them reading: With a few clicks, last-minute stress turns into thoughtful giving.

Unique Experiences vs Physical Gifts

Not every gift needs to be wrapped in paper. Sometimes the best presents are experiences that create memories. ChatGPT can help you compare both paths.

Example Prompt:
"Suggest 10 unique experience gifts for a couple in their 30s who love food and travel. Budget $100."

Sample Results:

- Tickets to a wine tasting event

- A cooking class for two
- A gift card for a weekend cabin rental
- A city walking tour with a local guide
- A meal delivery service trial

For Physical Gifts Prompt:
"Suggest 10 physical gifts for the same couple, same budget."

Why It Works: You get to weigh memory-making against something tangible. ChatGPT lets you see both sides and pick the one that fits.

Prompts to Spark Creativity

Sometimes the hardest part is just getting started. ChatGPT can be your spark.

Prompts to Try:

- "Give me 12 creative stocking stuffer ideas for coworkers. Keep them funny but appropriate."
- "Suggest 10 gifts for a book lover that are not books."
- "List 15 gift basket themes under $50. Include what to put inside."

- "Create a unique holiday gift idea for a teacher that students can help make."
- "Come up with 10 homemade gift ideas that use recycled or upcycled materials."

Why It Works: A list of possibilities gets your imagination moving. You may not use the exact suggestions, but they will inspire something even better.

Personalized Gift Ideas for Every Age and Budget

The best gifts feel personal. They show you what makes someone unique. ChatGPT can take a few details and generate dozens of ideas you never would have thought of.

Example Prompt:
"Give me 10 gift ideas for my dad who loves gardening, listens to jazz, and just retired. Keep each under $40."

Sample Results Might Include:

- A subscription to a jazz streaming service
- A sturdy pair of gardening gloves with wrist support
- A hardcover book of jazz history with photos

- A decorative plant stand for his back porch
- A weekend workshop on native plants at a local nursery

Another Prompt:
"My niece is turning 7. She loves unicorns, space, and drawing. Suggest 8 gifts under $25."

Why It Works: By adding details about age, interests, and budget, your chatbot becomes a gift concierge who never runs out of ideas.

Hook to keep them reading: You do not need to spend hours wandering the mall. One prompt can hand you the perfect list in seconds.

Last-Minute Gifts (Under $20, Printable, DIY)

We have all been there. A neighbor drops by with a plate of cookies and suddenly you need a gift to give back. ChatGPT can save you.

Example Prompt:
"**List 15 last-minute holiday gifts under $20 that I can buy today or print at home**."

Sample Results:

- Printable coupon for a coffee date
- A set of homemade spice mixes with recipe cards
- Digital puzzle or game app gift codes
- A festive holiday-scented candle
- DIY hot cocoa kit in a mason jar

DIY Twist:
Ask ChatGPT to generate simple instructions.
"Write easy steps for a homemade sugar scrub with ingredients I probably already have at home."

Why It Works: These quick solutions can be printed, cooked, or crafted in an hour. No panic, just joy.

Hook to keep them reading: With a few clicks, last-minute stress turns into thoughtful giving.

Unique Experiences vs Physical Gifts

Not every gift needs to be wrapped in paper. Sometimes the best presents are experiences that create memories. ChatGPT can help you compare both paths.

Example Prompt:
"**Suggest 10 unique experience gifts for a couple in their 30s who love food and travel. Budget $100**."

Sample Results:

- Tickets to a wine tasting event
- A cooking class for two
- A gift card for a weekend cabin rental
- A city walking tour with a local guide
- A meal delivery service trial

For Physical Gifts Prompt:
"Suggest 10 physical gifts for the same couple, same budget."

Why It Works: You get to weigh memory-making against something tangible. ChatGPT lets you see both sides and pick the one that fits.

Hook to keep them reading: A gift that becomes a story is one they will never forget.

Prompts to Spark Creativity

Sometimes the hardest part is just getting started. ChatGPT can be your spark.

Prompts to Try:

- "Give me 12 creative stocking stuffer ideas for coworkers. Keep them funny but appropriate."

- "Suggest 10 gifts for a book lover that are not books."
- "List 15 gift basket themes under $50. Include what to put inside."
- "Create a unique holiday gift idea for a teacher that students can help make."
- "Come up with 10 homemade gift ideas that use recycled or upcycled materials."

Why It Works: A list of possibilities gets your imagination moving. You may not use the exact suggestions, but they will inspire something even better.

The next chapter will carry these creative sparks into holidays all year long, so your Santa Bot keeps helping long after Christmas morning.

S.O.S. Santa: No Wrapping Paper? No Problem!

Picture this: It's Christmas Eve. The gifts are ready, the cocoa is hot, and you suddenly realize… no wrapping paper. Don't panic. Call in your Santa Bot and watch the magic happen.

Ask ChatGPT Prompt:
"I don't have wrapping paper. Give me 10 creative ways to wrap a holiday gift with things around the house."

Sample Santa-Approved Fixes:

- Scarves and Sweaters: Instant cozy wrapping, plus the wrap is part of the gift.
- Tinfoil or Parchment Paper: Shine like Rudolph's nose or look gourmet.
- Brown Paper Bags: Cut, flatten, and decorate with doodles, stamps, or ribbon.
- Old Maps or Sheet Music: Vintage charm that doubles as conversation starters.

- Newspaper Comics Section: Adds a retro, playful vibe.
- Coloring Book Pages: Blow up your favorites and turn them into wrapping or oversized gift tags.
- Pillowcases: Slip the gift inside and tie with ribbon. Done.

- Leftover Fabric Scraps: Make your gift look like it came from Santa's sewing room.
- Reusable Tote Bags: Two gifts in one.
- Giant Poster Prints from Walgreens or Office Supply Stores: Upload a fun design on Canva, print it out, and wrap big with big impact.

Why It Works: These solutions save you money, spark creativity, and turn wrapping into part of the gift itself.

Santa's Secret: The best wrapping is not perfect paper. It's the thought you put into it. And with ChatGPT on your side, Santa's always got a Plan B.

S.O.S. Santa: Guests Arrive Early

The doorbell rings, and you're still in your slippers. What now?

Ask ChatGPT Prompt:
"***Guests are arriving early. Give me 5 fun activities to keep them busy while I finish setting up.***"

Quick Fixes:

- Put kids in charge of a "holiday scavenger hunt" around the house.
- Hand out cookie cutters and let guests cut and decorate sugar cookies.
- Queue up a holiday trivia game (ChatGPT can generate the questions).
- Play "Guess the Carol" with just a few notes hummed.
- Give them a "photo booth corner" with hats, scarves, and props.

S.O.S. Santa: Turkey Trouble

Dinner disaster? Don't worry, Santa's Bot has your back.

Ask ChatGPT Prompt:
"***My turkey burned. What can I serve instead with what I already have in my pantry?"***

Quick Fixes:

- Shred a store-bought rotisserie chicken and serve with festive sides.
- Make "holiday sandwiches" with cranberry sauce, cheese, and bread.

- Create a pasta bake with leftover veggies and cream soup.
- Serve a cheese-and-fruit platter as a "fancy holiday meal."
- Own it: Call it "Santa's Smoky Feast" and laugh it off.

S.O.S. Santa: Forgot the Batteries

The kids are ready, the toys are not.

Ask ChatGPT Prompt:
"***No batteries and stores are closed. What are 5 creative ways to save the moment?***"

Quick Fixes:

- Wrap up a "Battery IOU" card with a funny poem.
- Switch focus to a family game or scavenger hunt.
- Turn the toy into part of a story: "Santa says it needs to charge with Christmas magic overnight."
- Distract with a "surprise snack bar" - popcorn, cocoa, and cookies.
- Swap batteries out of the remote (they'll forgive you).

S.O.S. Santa: Last-Minute Gift Panic

Forgot someone on your list? ChatGPT can help you whip up magic fast.

Ask ChatGPT Prompt:
"***Give me 10 last-minute holiday gift ideas I can create or deliver in under an hour.***"

Quick Fixes:

- A framed family photo printed at Walgreens.
- A "movie night in a bag" with popcorn, candy, and a streaming gift card.
- A hand-written coupon book: babysitting, errands, dog walking.
- A mason jar layered with cookie ingredients.
- A playlist of holiday songs curated just for them.

S.O.S. Santa: Out of Holiday Spirit

Even Santa gets tired sometimes.

Ask ChatGPT Prompt:

"I feel stressed and low on holiday spirit. Give me 5 ways to recharge quickly."

Quick Fixes:

- Step outside for five minutes of fresh air and starlight.
- Play your favorite carol and sing out loud.
- Write one quick gratitude list with three things you love.
- Watch a short funny holiday clip (ChatGPT can suggest some).
- Call a friend or family member just to say hi.
- Talk to your bot. Use the dictation tool on ChatGPT and share your thoughts and issues.

Chapter 3. Beyond Christmas: Holidays All Year

The sparkle of Christmas lights may fade in January, but life keeps offering reasons to gather, give, and celebrate.

ChatGPT can carry the holiday spirit into every season, becoming a helper that works year-round. Let's take a look at how your Santa Bot can step into other traditions and special days.

The glow of the Christmas tree fades, the wrapping paper has been recycled, and the stockings are tucked away.

But guess what?

Life keeps giving us reasons to celebrate. From New Year's fireworks to Valentine's hearts, ChatGPT can be your year-round celebration partner.

This chapter will show you how to use your Santa Bot for every season, every milestone, and every toast you might need to give.

Thanksgiving Gratitude and Gathering

Thanksgiving is all about food, family, and gratitude. The stress often comes from menu planning and making sure no one leaves the table disappointed.

Thanksgiving can feel like a full-time job. The guest list, the turkey, the pies, the side dishes, the seating charts. But your chatbot can help lighten that load.

- **Meal Planning**: Ask for menus that serve a crowd, including vegetarian or gluten-free options.
- **Shopping Lists**: Generate your grocery list instantly.

- **Gratitude Prompts**: Have ChatGPT create a “thankful game” for the dinner table, with fun prompts like, “Name one invention you couldn’t live without” or “Tell a story about kindness.”

How ChatGPT helps:

- Create a shopping list from your recipes in seconds.
- Suggest three side dishes that fit a guest’s dietary needs.

- Write a short gratitude message you can read before the meal.
- Plan cooking timelines so the turkey and the rolls are ready together.

Prompt to try:
"***Help me create a Thanksgiving menu for 8 people. One person is vegan and one person is gluten-free. Give me a shopping list organized by grocery store section.***"

New Year's Eve Fresh Starts and Fireworks

Just days after Christmas, New Year's Eve sneaks up on everyone. Whether you want a quiet reflection or a lively party, ChatGPT can help you close out the year right.

Instead of writing vague resolutions, let your Santa Bot help make them achievable.

- **Resolution Maker**: Ask for goals broken into small, do-able steps.

- **Party Planner**: Generate themed party ideas, countdown playlists, and midnight toast scripts.
- **Reflection Journal**: Get end-of-year reflection prompts for your family or for yourself.

Prompt to try:

"Write five fun but realistic New Year's resolutions for a busy parent who wants more peace, more laughter, and a healthier lifestyle."

How ChatGPT helps:

- Draft resolutions that are realistic and fun.
- Create trivia questions about the past year for your party.
- Suggest drink or mocktail menus.
- Write a quick thank-you toast to friends who helped you this year.

Prompt to try:
"***Write a short but inspiring New Year's toast for friends at a small dinner. Keep it lighthearted but meaningful.***"

Hanukkah Eight Nights of Light

Eight nights mean eight opportunities to plan meals, tell stories, and light candles with intention.

Hanukkah brings families together around tradition, light, and joy. ChatGPT can help keep the celebration meaningful and fresh.

- **Gift Ideas**: Plan small, thoughtful gifts for each of the eight nights.
- **Recipes**: Find variations of latkes or sufganiyot to try.
- **Storytelling**: Ask for age-appropriate retellings of the Hanukkah story for kids.

How ChatGPT helps:

- Write explanations of Hanukkah traditions for kids or guests new to the holiday.
- Suggest small, meaningful gift ideas for each night.
- Generate themed trivia questions or riddles.
- Provide recipes with variations, like dairy-free latkes or gluten-free sufganiyot.

Prompt to try:
"Give me 8 small Hanukkah gift ideas under $20 for a 10-year-old who loves reading and art."

Kwanzaa Principles and Connection

Celebrated from December 26 to January 1, Kwanzaa emphasizes values like unity, creativity, and faith.

Kwanzaa is about unity, creativity, and reflection. Your chatbot can help create activities that highlight each principle.

- **Daily Activities**: Ask for ideas tied to Umoja (unity) or Kuumba (creativity).
- **Decor Inspiration**: Generate table setting or room décor ideas inspired by Kwanzaa colors and symbols.
- **Community Sharing**: Write a reflection to share with family each night.

How ChatGPT helps:

- Create family activities around each principle (Nguzo Saba).
- Write a daily reflection or journal prompt.
- Suggest simple, symbolic crafts to honor the traditions.
- Provide African-inspired recipes that fit a family dinner.

Prompt to try:
"***Suggest 7 family discussion questions for Kwanzaa, one for each principle.***"

Día de los Reyes (Three Kings Day) The Gift of the Kings

Celebrated in many Spanish-speaking cultures, January 6 marks the arrival of the Three Kings. Children leave shoes out for gifts, and families share rosca de reyes.

Gift Planning: Create simple ideas for small shoe gifts.

Storytelling: Retell the Three Kings' story for younger children.

Crafts: Ask for crown-making activities with paper or cardboard.

On January 6, many families celebrate the arrival of the Three Wise Men. This holiday extends the magic of Christmas and often involves sweet bread, gifts, and community gatherings.

How ChatGPT helps:

- Write stories retelling the journey of the Three Kings for children.
- Suggest small, affordable gifts tied to the tradition.
- Plan a festive breakfast menu with Rosca de Reyes and hot chocolate.
- Create thank-you notes for teachers or neighbors that tie into the theme of giving.

Prompt to try:
"***Write a bedtime story for kids about the journey of the Three Wise Men"*** *or*

"Give me five fun activities for kids to celebrate Día de los Reyes at home, with low-cost materials."

Valentine's Day: Love Notes and Sweet Surprises

By mid-February, hearts and roses take over the stores. With your bot's help, you can skip the cliché and go straight to heartfelt.

- **Love Letters**: Generate a custom poem or note.
- **Creative Gifts**: Brainstorm "experience" gifts like a picnic or handmade coupon book.

- **School Cards**: Print playful, pun-filled cards for kids' classmates.

Prompt to try:

"***Write 10 Valentine's card messages for kids, each with a fun pun about animals.***"

Birthday Hacks with ChatGPT

Birthdays happen year-round, and they sneak up on us. Your chatbot can be your reminder and your helper.

- **Party Themes**: Ask for kid or adult party themes tailored to interests.

- **Gift Ideas**: Get gift lists based on age, hobbies, and budget.
- **Cake Alternatives**: Brainstorm fun dessert ideas beyond the usual cake.

Prompt to try:

"***Give me 5 creative birthday party themes for a 10-year-old who loves space, video games, and pizza.***"

Greetings and Toasts for Every Occasion

Sometimes the hardest part of a celebration is finding the right words. ChatGPT can give you options — heartfelt, funny, formal, or casual.

- **Toasts**: For weddings, birthdays, retirements, or family dinners.
- **Cards**: Sympathy, congratulations, or encouragement cards.
- **Social Media**: Posts that hit the right tone.

Prompt to try:

"***Write a short, warm toast for my best friend's birthday dinner that mixes humor and sincerity.***"

The truth is, Christmas may be the glittering centerpiece of the holiday season, but your Santa Bot can work just as hard for every other celebration that fills the year.

When you use ChatGPT as your behind-the-scenes helper, every holiday feels a little lighter, a little brighter, and a lot less stressful.

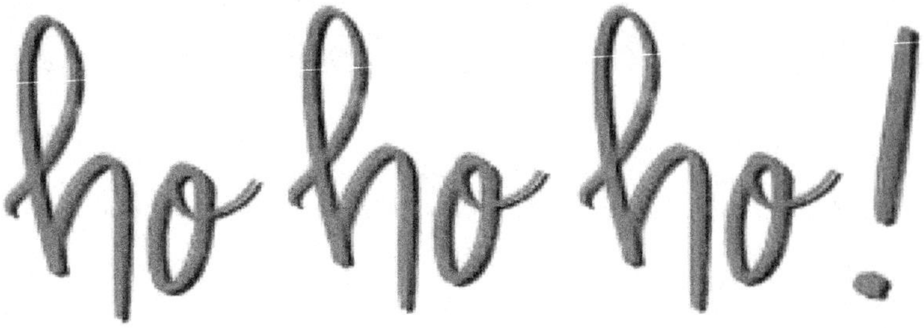

Chapter 4. Invitations, Letters, and Cards

When the holidays roll around, the paper trail (and digital trail) starts to pile up. Holiday letters, greeting cards, invitations, RSVPs, thank-yous - it's a lot.

This is where your ChatGPT Santa Bot shines. It can spin your scattered thoughts into words that sound warm, polished, or even hilarious - whatever tone you want.

Think of your Santa Bot as the holiday wordsmith you didn't know you had. You feed it the details, and it gives you something that looks like you spent hours writing.

Write the Perfect Holiday Letter

The annual holiday letter has been both loved and dreaded for decades. Some families want to celebrate every milestone. Others just want to share a funny story or keep it short. Either way, ChatGPT can help you hit the right note.

Here's how:

Prompt:
"Write a one-page holiday letter in a warm, friendly tone. Mention that our family adopted a puppy, our

daughter started high school, and we took a road trip to the Grand Canyon. End with a message of gratitude and joy for the year ahead."

Sample Output:

Dear friends and family,
What a year it has been! Our biggest joy was welcoming our new puppy, Daisy, who has already chewed through three pairs of shoes and stolen every heart in the house. Emily started high school this fall, and we couldn't be prouder watching her dive into choir and make new friends. We also piled into the car this summer for a road trip to the Grand Canyon - breathtaking views, countless trail snacks, and only a few "are we there yet?" moments. We are grateful for the love and laughter that carried us through the year, and we look forward to the joy that 2026 will bring. Wishing you and yours peace, health, and plenty of cookies.

Funny vs Heartfelt Card Prompts

Not everyone wants a serious card. Sometimes the best way to connect is with humor. ChatGPT can give you both sides - the Hallmark and the Comedy Club.

Prompt for Funny Card:
"Write a funny one-liner for a Christmas card about how chaotic the holidays feel in our house with three kids under ten."

Sample Funny Card Line:
"All is calm, all is bright… just kidding. Nothing is calm, and someone just spilled cocoa on the cat."

Prompt for Heartfelt Card:
"Write a heartfelt Christmas card message for my best friend who has been my support all year."

Sample Heartfelt Card Line:
"Your friendship has been the gift that carried me through 2025. May your holiday be filled with the love and warmth you've shared so generously with me."

Invitations with RSVP Wording

If you've ever stared at a blank screen thinking, *How do I make this sound fun but not tacky?* — that's exactly where your Santa Bot comes in.

Prompt:
"Write a short invitation to a holiday dinner for neighbors. Make it cheerful and include RSVP wording."

Sample Invitation:
Please join us for a cozy holiday dinner!
When: Saturday, December 14th at 6 PM
Where: The McMillan Home, 123 Pine Street
Bring your appetite and your holiday cheer. Kindly RSVP by December 7th so we can save you a seat at the table.

SOS Santa Tip: Out of time? Ask ChatGPT to *"Write a text-friendly version of this invite in under 50 words."* Copy, paste, send. Done.

Thank-You Notes Made Simple

Handwritten or digital, thank-you notes never go out of style. They show appreciation and keep the holiday spirit alive even after the tree comes down. ChatGPT can help you strike the right balance of sincere and quick.

Prompt:
"Write a short thank-you note for receiving homemade cookies from a neighbor. Keep it warm and friendly."

Sample Thank-You Note:

Dear Anna,
Your cookies were pure holiday magic! We devoured them in one evening, and the cinnamon-ginger ones disappeared first. Thank you for thinking of us — you made our season sweeter in every way.

Prompt:
"Write a thank-you note for a gift card from a relative I don't see very often."

Sample Thank-You Note:
Dear Uncle Mark,
Thank you so much for the thoughtful gift card. It's always nice to treat ourselves after the busy holiday rush, and your kindness makes it even more special. We're sending love and warm wishes your way this season.

Wrapping Up the Words

Invitations, letters, cards, thank-yous - they can all feel like one more pile on the holiday to-do list. But with ChatGPT, you don't have to start from scratch. You just tell your Santa Bot the details, and it handles the writing elves' work.

Santa's SOS Box:

- Out of wrapping paper? Print a holiday poster at Walgreens.
- No card handy? Ask your bot for a one-liner you can text.
- Forgot to say thank you? Ask for a note that sounds warm and personal.

Words matter at the holidays. ChatGPT makes sure your's feel festive, heartfelt, and ready on time.

Chapter 5. New Traditions and Family Fun

The best holidays are not the ones with the perfect turkey or the perfectly wrapped gifts. They're the ones with laughter, shared stories, and little traditions that turn into memories. Y

our Santa Bot can help you create those magical moments without the stress of inventing them all from scratch.

Think of ChatGPT as a holiday idea machine that never runs out of spark. Whether you need a brand-new family tradition, a bedtime story to settle kids after too much sugar, or a scavenger hunt to keep guests entertained, your Santa Bot has you covered.

Creating Stories and Games with ChatGPT

Nothing brings a family closer than a shared story or a goofy game. You don't have to be a writer or a game designer to create something wonderful. Just tell your Santa Bot who's playing and what vibe you want.

Prompt:
"Write a 5-minute silly game for four people at Christmas dinner. Use napkins, spoons, or anything on the table."

Sample Game:
Holiday Hat Trick - Everyone folds their napkin into a "hat." Place the hat on your head and balance a spoon on top. The first person to keep both on for 30 seconds while humming "Jingle Bells" wins a candy cane.

Prompt:
"Create a short holiday story where Grandma is a superhero who saves Christmas dinner."

Sample Story Idea:
Grandma grabs her rolling pin cape and dashes into the kitchen when the oven breaks down. With a wave of her "magic ladle," she turns mashed potatoes into a feast fit for kings. The whole family cheers, and Grandma becomes the star of Christmas Eve.

Holiday Bedtime Stories for Kids

Sometimes kids need a calm-down after all the excitement. ChatGPT can spin a gentle story in seconds — tailored to their favorite toys, pets, or wishes.

Prompt:
"Tell a short, cozy bedtime story for a 4-year-old about a teddy bear who goes on a snowy adventure with the family dog."

Sample Story Start:
Once upon a frosty night, Teddy Bear slipped on his red scarf and tiptoed outside. Snowflakes tickled his nose as the family dog trotted up, wagging his tail. Together they followed the trail of sparkling stars to find the secret Christmas tree hidden in the forest.

You can even ask for **illustration prompts** to use with crayons or markers so kids can draw along with the story.

Family Trivia and Scavenger Hunts

Turn ordinary gatherings into playful adventures. ChatGPT can help you create trivia games about your own family or scavenger hunts that make everyone laugh.

Prompt:
"Write 10 trivia questions for a holiday game night. Mix easy ones for kids and harder ones for adults."

Sample Trivia:

- *What reindeer's name starts with a "V"?*
- *Which holiday dessert is also called a yule log?*
- *Which year was the first iPhone released?*

Prompt:
"Create a Christmas scavenger hunt list for indoors. Keep it lighthearted and silly."

Sample Hunt Items:

- Find something red that jingles
- Find a cookie crumb (bonus if it's on Santa's plate)
- Find the funniest ornament on the tree
- Find a gift with the shiniest wrapping

SOS Santa Tip: *If your house feels too quiet, a scavenger hunt or trivia game is an instant cure.*

Digital Scrapbooks / Memory Books

After the laughter, you'll want a way to capture the joy. ChatGPT can help you create a scrapbook template, a family memory book, or even a digital slideshow with captions.

Prompt:
"Create 10 memory prompts for a family scrapbook about this Christmas."

Sample Prompts:

- *The funniest thing that happened at dinner was…*
- *The gift that surprised me most was…*
- *The person who made me laugh the hardest was…*
- *If this holiday had a theme song, it would be…*

You can print these prompts on slips of paper, pass them around, and collect responses to include in a scrapbook. Or drop them into Canva to make a photo book in minutes.

SOS Santa Tip: *Not a crafter? No problem. Take smartphone photos, ask your bot to write captions, and upload them to a photo service. Instant scrapbook.*

Wrapping It Up

Traditions don't have to be passed down for centuries. They can start today. Whether it's a silly game with spoons, a bedtime story about a teddy bear, or a scrapbook of everyone's favorite moments, your Santa Bot can make it happen.

This holiday, give yourself permission to invent something new. Who knows? The little tradition you start tonight may be the one your kids or grandkids carry on for decades.

Chapter 6. Parties and Gatherings

The holidays have always been about gathering - from the feasts of ancient Rome to the candlelit banquets of the Middle Ages to the twinkling parties of the Victorian age. People crave warmth, light, and laughter when the days grow shorter. Today, your Santa Bot can help you carry on that tradition, making your gatherings not just meals but memories.

Menu Planning and Grocery Lists

Every great party starts with food. Whether you're serving turkey, tamales, or takeout, your Santa Bot can make the planning simple.

Prompt:
"Plan a Christmas Eve menu for 10 people, with one vegetarian and two kids. Include a shopping list."

Sample Menu:

- Roast chicken with rosemary
- Vegetarian lasagna
- Green beans with toasted almonds

- Mashed potatoes and gravy
- Kid-friendly mac and cheese
- Chocolate yule log

The shopping list is generated instantly, saving you hours of hunting through cookbooks. You can even ask for **make-ahead tips** so you spend less time in the kitchen and more time with your guests.

SOS Santa Tip: Out of nutmeg at the last minute? Ask your bot for substitutions. Cinnamon and a pinch of cloves can give you the same cozy flavor.

Seating Charts and Conversation Starters

Holiday dinners can be tricky. Who sits next to whom? How do you avoid awkward silence?

Prompt:
"Create a seating chart for 8 people at Christmas dinner. Place chatty relatives between quiet ones."

Your Santa Bot can balance the table so Grandma isn't stuck next to the teen glued to their phone, and Uncle Bob gets a seat across from someone who can actually stand his stories.

For conversation starters, just ask.

Prompt:
"Give me 10 fun holiday questions to ask at the table."

Sample Questions:

- If you could invite any historical figure to Christmas dinner, who would it be?
- What's the best gift you've ever received?
- If your life had a holiday movie soundtrack, what song would play?

Playlist Suggestions by Mood

Music sets the tone. Think of the carols sung in candlelit churches centuries ago, or the jazz and swing that defined Christmas in the 1940s. A good playlist can wrap the room in nostalgia or energy.

Prompt:
"Make a playlist for a cozy Christmas Eve by the fire."

Sample Playlist Idea:

- "Silent Night" (instrumental piano)

- “Have Yourself a Merry Little Christmas” (Judy Garland)
- “The Christmas Song” (Nat King Cole)
- “River” (Joni Mitchell)

Prompt:
"Make a playlist for a high-energy New Year’s Eve party."

Sample Playlist Idea:

- “Auld Lang Syne” remix
- “Happy” (Pharrell Williams)
- “Don’t Stop Believin’” (Journey)
- “Uptown Funk” (Bruno Mars)

With ChatGPT, you can even design playlists by *decade*, *genre*, or *theme*.

Icebreakers and Games

Parties shine when guests feel relaxed. That’s where your Santa Bot earns its stripes.

Prompt:
"Give me 5 holiday icebreaker games for adults at a dinner party."

Sample Games:

- **Holiday Pictionary**: draw Christmas songs on napkins.
- **Guess the Gift**: wrap a silly object and have guests shake, poke, or smell it to guess.
- **Two Truths and a Lie: Holiday Edition**: share three Christmas memories, one false.

SOS Santa Tip: Kids restless? Ask your bot to make a scavenger hunt or holiday charades game on the fly.

Wrapping It Up

For centuries, the holidays have been about gathering to eat, drink, and make merry. Now, with your Santa Bot, you don't need a team of servants or weeks of planning. You can create a feast, a seating plan, a playlist, and even a game night in minutes.

The glow of candles, the hum of conversation, the music drifting through the air - these are the treasures of a holiday well spent. And with a little AI magic, you can focus on what matters most: being present with the people you love.

Chapter 7. Travel Made Easy

The holidays are meant to sparkle, but travel can dim the glow fast. Packed airports, restless kids, icy roads, and forgotten toothbrushes - it all adds up.

The good news? With a little planning and a friendly chatbot by your side, travel becomes smoother, safer, and even fun.

Packing Lists for Families

Packing feels endless: clothes, shoes, toiletries, electronics, gifts. It's easy to forget socks while remembering three chargers. That's where your Santa Bot saves the day.

Prompt:
"Make a packing list for a family of four traveling by car for 5 days over Christmas. Include clothes, toiletries, electronics, gifts, and comfort items."

Sample Essentials:

- Clothes: layers, pajamas, dressy outfits, extra socks, warm coats
- Toiletries: toothbrushes, toothpaste, shampoo, lip balm, tissues
- Electronics: chargers, power bank, headphones
- Gifts: wrapped and labeled, plus a roll of tape and scissors
- Comfort: pillows, blankets, slippers, favorite snacks

SOS Santa Tip: Always pack one **"go bag"** for emergencies — extra clothes, water bottles, and a small first-aid kit.

Entertainment for Kids on the Road

Nothing stretches time like a car full of kids asking, “Are we there yet?” Your Santa Bot can give you a treasure chest of ideas.

Prompt:
"Suggest 10 holiday-themed car games for kids ages 6 to 10."

Sample Games:

- **Holiday I Spy**: “I spy something red and shiny” (a Rudolph nose).
- **Santa’s Alphabet**: go through the alphabet spotting words on signs.
- **Christmas Song Bingo**: print a sheet with holiday songs; mark them off as they play on the radio.
- **Story Swap**: each person adds a sentence to a silly Christmas tale.

Load up audiobooks, podcasts or custom bedtime stories written by ChatGPT for cozy travel moments.

SOS Santa Tip: Keep a small basket of surprise toys or snacks in the front seat. Hand one back when tensions rise.

Route Planning with Backup Options

Weather, traffic, or surprise construction can turn the best-laid plans upside down.

A smart traveler always has a Plan B.

Prompt:
"Plan a driving route from Dallas to Denver for Christmas, avoiding tolls, with two backup options if there's bad weather."

Ideas:

- Primary: fastest interstate with rest stops every 90 miles
- Backup A: scenic route with small towns and gas stations
- Backup B: short detour routes marked for icy road warnings

Check the weather before leaving. Ask your bot:
"What's the 3-day forecast for my route, and what hazards should I expect?"

SOS Santa Tip: Keep a blanket, shovel, and flashlight in the trunk. You'll probably never need them — but if you do, you'll be glad.

Polite Cancellation Texts

Sometimes the storm wins. Flights are grounded, cars can't make it, and you're stuck at home. ChatGPT helps soften the blow.

Prompt:
"Write a kind text to my sister explaining that snow has canceled our trip, and we'll do a video call instead."

Sample Texts:

- "We're so sad we can't make it through the storm, but we'll be with you in spirit and on Zoom at 6. Save us a cookie!"
- "The roads are icy and we don't want to risk it. Let's reschedule our hugs for New Year's — love you."

You can also ask for **formal messages** if it's work-related travel.

Comfort on the Road

Small things matter on long journeys. Before you leave, think comfort.

- **Shoes**: Driving in high heels or stiff boots? Pack easy slip-ons.
- **Clothes**: Layer up - cozy sweaters, stretchy pants, warm socks.
- **Snacks**: Granola bars, peanut butter sandwiches, trail mix, fruit, water. Skip too much sugar.
- **Music**: A holiday playlist to keep spirits bright.
- **Stops**: Plan bathroom and meal breaks before you hear the backseat revolt.
- **Bring a blanket,** which makes for great car naps.

Prompt:
"Give me a checklist for a road trip survival kit for winter holidays."

Sample List:

- Travel pillow
- Reusable water bottles

- Hand wipes
- Car charger
- Extra blanket
- Umbrella
- Small trash bags
- A towel

Wrapping It Up

Travel doesn't have to be chaos. With planning prompts, backup routes, and creative entertainment, the road to Grandma's house can feel less like a chore and more like part of the holiday fun. When the weather snarls or kids get restless, you'll be ready.

Picture it: laughter bubbling from the backseat, hot cocoa in the cup holder, twinkle lights glowing in passing towns. That's holiday travel at its best - and with a little AI magic, it can be yours.

Chapter 8. Decor and DIY Crafts

Decorating is where the holiday magic comes alive. A tree that sparkles in the corner, a wreath on the door, a table set with candles and evergreens — these touches create the glow that makes a season feel unforgettable. The good news is you don't need to break the bank or run to ten different stores. Your Santa Bot can help you pick a theme, find materials, and even walk you through the craft projects step by step.

Decorating Themes and Color Palettes

Every holiday season comes with new trends. Some years it's all white-and-gold elegance, others it's rustic plaids and farmhouse charm. Maybe you're drawn to neon lights and bold metallics.

Prompt:
"Give me 5 Christmas decorating themes with matching color palettes and suggested materials for each."

Sample Results:

- **Classic Red & Green**: red bows, pine garlands, shiny green ornaments.
- **Nordic Cozy**: whites, grays, wood textures, wool stockings.
- **Glam Gold**: metallic gold ornaments, glittered pinecones, champagne table runners.
- **Whimsical Candyland**: bright pink, turquoise, candy canes, gingerbread figures.
- **Rustic Lodge**: plaid blankets, lanterns, faux fur pillows, natural pinecones.

SOS Santa Tip: If you're not sure where to shop, ask: *"Find local stores near (your town) that sell farmhouse-style holiday décor under $50."*

ChatGPT can also suggest **resale shops, estate sales, or craft supply swaps** in your community.

Printable Tags and Ornaments

Handmade touches make gifts and trees feel special. You don't need a fancy printer — just some cardstock, scissors, and a little imagination.

Prompt:
"Make me a printable gift tag template with Santa hats and space for To/From."

You can also ask:
"Suggest 10 ornament designs I can make from felt and buttons with kids."

Use Canva or even Word templates, then print them at your local Walgreens or office supply store. These make great classroom projects or office gift exchanges.

SOS Santa Tip: Out of wrapping paper? Print a giant poster at your local copy shop with a holiday design and use it as one-of-a-kind paper. ChatGPT will generate patterns for you.

DIY Wreaths, Table Settings and Centerpieces

A wreath can be made from almost anything - ribbon scraps, twigs, even old ornaments. ChatGPT can guide you step by step.

Prompt:
"Write step-by-step instructions for a DIY wreath using dollar store supplies."

Sample Table Setting Ideas:

- Mason jars filled with tea lights.
- Pine branches down the center with cranberries sprinkled in.
- Vintage books stacked with candles on top.
- Candy canes tied together to make napkin rings.

Centerpieces don't need to be expensive. Ask your bot for **budget-friendly centerpieces under $15.**

Photo Booth Prompts

Memories matter as much as meals. A simple corner with a backdrop and a box of props turns any gathering into a party.

Prompt:
"Give me 15 holiday photo booth ideas with props I can make at home."

Examples:

- Santa hats on sticks.
- Elf ears cut from cardboard.
- A giant candy cane frame.
- A snowy backdrop made from cotton batting.

SOS Santa Tip: Ask ChatGPT: *"What are 5 funny captions to use for a holiday photo booth sign?"*

Lights, Storage and Smart Setups

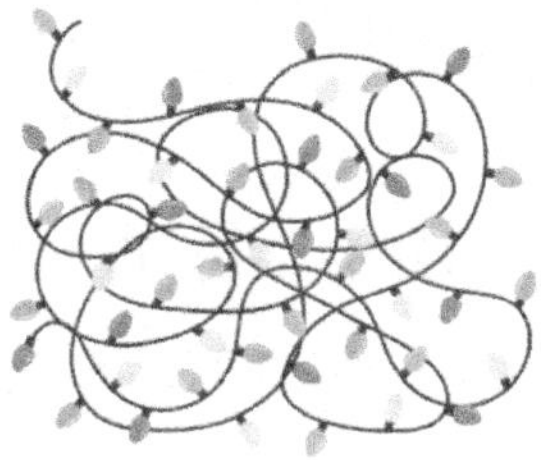

Don't let tangled lights steal your January joy. Your Santa Bot can show you the best ways to store lights, ornaments, and garlands.

Prompt:
"Give me 10 clever ways to store Christmas lights so they don't tangle."

Sample Tips:

- Wrap around cardboard rectangles.
- Coil into old coffee cans.
- Use plastic hangers as spools.
- Store by room in clear bins with labels.

And when you're setting them up? Ask for help sizing:

"How many feet of lights do I need for a 7-foot Christmas tree*?"*

Answer: About 500–600 lights for a medium coverage tree.

Hire a Pro to Light Your Home

And don't forget the outside of your home. Many neighborhoods now sparkle with professional light displays. ChatGPT can help you find local companies that offer outdoor decorating services, compare their prices, read reviews, and even suggest the best times to book before the season rush.

Just ask:
"Find five outdoor holiday lighting companies near

me, compare reviews and prices, and suggest the best choice for a mid-size home."

This way you can enjoy the glow without climbing a ladder yourself.

Wrapping It Up

Decor doesn't need to be expensive or exhausting. With a few prompts, you can find your color palette, print your own ornaments, or craft a wreath that looks store-bought. ChatGPT can even locate coupons, local stores, and online tutorials so you can focus on making the season bright.

Think of it as your holiday decorator on demand. Whether you want magazine-perfect glam or homespun cozy charm, you'll have ideas at your fingertips. And when it's time to pack it all away, you'll know exactly how to do it without the dreaded January mess.

Chapter 9. Side Hustles and Holiday Cash

The holidays are magical, but they can also be expensive. Between gifts, travel, food, and decorations, budgets get stretched. The good news is that ChatGPT can help you find creative ways to *save money, earn money, and spend money smarter.* Think of this chapter as your "North Pole Workshop for the Wallet."

Seasonal Gig Ideas

When money gets tight, a short-term seasonal gig can fill the stockings. ChatGPT can brainstorm seasonal jobs in your town and help you compare options.

Ideas to ask about:

- Gift wrapping at malls or boutiques
- Working at holiday markets, craft fairs, or pop-up shops
- Driving deliveries for local bakeries, caterers, or Amazon seasonal routes
- Caroling groups or Santa photography assistants
- Dog walking or pet sitting when families travel

Prompt to try:
"List 10 seasonal side jobs in (your area) that pay at least $15 an hour and require no long-term contract."

Selling Crafts, Printables, or Services

If you're creative, ChatGPT can help you turn that talent into extra holiday cash. From crafts to digital downloads, the market is wide.

Examples:

- Handmade ornaments or stockings
- Printable calendars, planners, or party games
- Custom gift baskets
- Services like decorating trees or setting up outdoor lights

Prompt to try:
"Write a friendly Etsy description for handmade cinnamon ornaments that emphasizes holiday nostalgia and makes them a perfect stocking stuffer."

Bake, Share and Sell

Food is one of the biggest holiday hustles. If you're overloaded with work, ChatGPT can help you locate bakers or tamale makers in your community.

Prompts to try:

- ***"Search for local bakers offering holiday cookie boxes under $40 near (your area)."***
- ***"List community Facebook groups where I can post that I'm selling homemade tamales for Christmas."***

Flip the script: If you love baking, ChatGPT can write an ad, design a flyer, or even draft a business card.

Prompt to try:
"Write a fun Facebook Marketplace post advertising homemade tamales, including pickup times and a holiday special of buy 5 dozen get 1 free."

Hire and Be Hired

Side hustles aren't just about what you can sell - it's also about what you can outsource to save time and reduce stress.

Think of the tasks you dread:

- Wrapping endless gifts
- Hanging lights
- Deep cleaning before guests arrive
- Driving kids to extra practices or parties

ChatGPT can write a quick neighborhood ad, a polite "help wanted" message, or even suggest reasonable rates. You're giving yourself time back, which may be the most valuable gift of the season.

Prompt to try:
"Write a short ad to hire a high school student to wrap 50 presents for $75, including materials provided."

Time Management Hacks for Hustlers

If you decide to launch your own holiday hustle, time is your biggest challenge. ChatGPT can help you plan schedules, track orders, and manage communication.

Prompts to try:

- ***"Make a 2-week baking schedule for 20 dozen cookies with delivery dates and ingredient shopping lists."***
- ***"Write an email template to confirm a tamale order with customer pickup details."***

Santa's Side Hustle Box

When in doubt, ask your Santa Bot for both sides of the hustle:

- Where can I find help?
- How can I offer help?

The holiday season is about community sharing skills, and making sure everyone's stockings are full, whether with money saved, money earned, or simply time gifted back to you.

Chapter 10. Faith, Reflection, and Self-Care

The holidays often shine with joy, but they can also stir up stress, loneliness, or memories that weigh heavy. Taking care of yourself is just as important as buying gifts or hosting guests.

Think of this chapter as a gentle pause in the middle of the season - a space where you can breathe, reflect, and recharge your holiday spirit.

Writing Prayers, Blessings, and Meditations

For many people, faith is the anchor of the season. Whether you attend church regularly, or simply hold quiet moments of reflection, ChatGPT can help you create personalized words that speak to your heart.

Examples:

- A short blessing before a holiday meal
- A bedtime meditation to ease children into peaceful sleep
- A written prayer of gratitude for family and friends

Prompts to try:

- ***"Write a short non-denominational blessing for Christmas dinner with family of mixed faiths."***
- ***"Create a 5-minute meditation script that focuses on peace and calm during the busy holiday season."***
- ***"Write a bedtime prayer for children that emphasizes kindness, gratitude, and joy."***

Gratitude Journals and Family Reflections

One of the most powerful stress relievers is gratitude. Journaling doesn't have to be a long daily essay — just a sentence or two about what went right. ChatGPT can give you prompts if you're stuck.

Prompts to try:

- ***"Give me 5 journal prompts for reflecting on my favorite holiday memories."***
- ***"Help me list 10 things I can be grateful for when my family dynamics feel stressful."***
- ***"Write a short reflection on how small acts of kindness can transform the holiday season."***

You can also ask your Santa Bot to create family reflection questions for the dinner table or a quiet night by the tree.

Examples:

- “What was the best gift you gave someone this year?”
- “What moment made you laugh the hardest this season?”
- “What tradition would you like to start next year?”

Boundaries: How to Say No With Grace

The holidays often bring pressure — extra parties, requests for money, and last-minute favors. Saying “no” doesn’t make you a Scrooge. It keeps you healthy.

ChatGPT can draft graceful responses so you can protect your time and peace of mind without guilt.

Prompts to try:

- ***"Write a polite decline for a holiday party invitation when I need rest."***

- ***"Draft a message saying I cannot contribute financially this year but I am still supportive."***
- ***"Give me 5 short ways to say no kindly but firmly when asked to take on more holiday tasks."***

Boundaries are the wrapping paper around your well-being. They protect what's inside.

Stress Relief Prompts for Calm Holidays

Daily self-care is not optional. Even ten minutes outside under the big sky can clear your head. Fresh air, sunlight, and movement are natural medicines for winter stress.

ChatGPT can help you create routines:

- Morning affirmations
- Gentle yoga or stretching plans
- Mindful breathing exercises
- End-of-day reflection prompts

Prompts to try:

- ***"Create a 7-day holiday self-care plan with one small activity each day."***

- ***"Write three affirmations to repeat when I feel overwhelmed by family dynamics."***
- ***"List five quick stress-relief techniques I can do in the car before going into a busy gathering."***

Santa's SOS for the Heart

If you feel low, lonely, or simply drained, don't wait until the season is over to ask for help. Use your Santa Bot for gentle support.

SOS Prompts:

- *"Remind me why the holidays matter when I feel down."*
- *"Write a message I can send to a friend asking if they'd like to meet for coffee because I'm feeling isolated."*
- *"Suggest calming activities I can do alone on Christmas Day to feel less lonely."*

And remember - your bot can even help you find real-world support.

Prompts to try:

- ***"Find local churches or community groups near me with holiday services."***
- ***"List community centers offering free or low-cost events this week."***
- ***"Suggest conversation starters if I'm nervous about attending a new group or service."***

Closing Reflection

The holidays are about giving, but don't forget to give yourself rest, peace, and space to reflect.

ChatGPT can act as a gentle guide, helping you write, breathe, pray, and say no when you need to. The gift of self-care may be the most powerful gift you can unwrap this season.

Chapter 11. Crisis Helper

Let's start with a quick laugh.

Q: What's the best way to keep your turkey from drying out this holiday season?
A: Invite your in-laws - nothing dries out faster than their approval.

Holidays can feel like a pressure cooker. The good news is you have a built-in helper at your fingertips: *your chatbot*.

Whether it's a burnt turkey, last-minute guests, or feeling guilty after one too many slices of pie, ChatGPT can step in as a calm voice, an idea machine, and a reset button.

Burnt Turkey Fixes

Creative Cooking Prompts:

Ask your bot, "***My turkey is overcooked and dry. What fast side dish or sauce can rescue it?***"

You'll get ideas like gravy hacks, cranberry compote, or shredding the turkey for tacos.

Menu Expansion:

Prompt: "Give me 3 ways to repurpose overcooked turkey into new dishes." You'll not only save dinner but maybe even impress your guests.

Guest Cancellations

Reframe the Moment:

Canceled guests can feel disappointing. Try a gratitude prompt: "***Help me list five good things about fewer people showing up."***

Meal Adjustments: Ask your bot how to scale downside dishes, repurpose food for freezer meals, or package leftovers as gifts.

Last-Minute Gift Ideas

Gift Generator: Prompt: "***Give me thoughtful under-$25 gift ideas for an uncle who loves fishing."***

DIY Inspiration: Ask: ***"What quick DIY gifts can I make with common household items?"***

Digital Lifesavers: Bots can suggest instant gifts like e-books, subscriptions, or custom playlists.

"Sorry We're Late" Texts

Holiday travel is unpredictable.

Prompt: ***"Write me a polite text to send to my aunt since we're running 45 minutes late."***

Or, lighten the mood: "Write a funny excuse about getting lost between the living room and the garage."

Balancing Food and Drink

Holiday spreads are tempting. Your bot can help with balance without judgment.

Meal Plans: "***Help me make a lighter breakfast since I know dinner will be heavy.***"

Mindful Reminders: "***Give me a gentle reminder prompt for portion control during parties."***

Next-Day Recovery: "***Suggest a day-after detox menu with simple meals and hydration tips."***

Work Doesn't Pause for Holidays

Many people juggle deadlines and family traditions at the same time.

Micro-Tasks: Ask your bot: "***Help me break my unfinished project into three 10-minute tasks.***"

Email Templates: "***Write me a cheerful but professional out-of-office email.***"

Boundary Prompts: "***Help me draft a polite message saying I'll respond after the holiday.***"

Planners, Schedules and Staying Calm

You don't need to buy a whole new system — your bot can build one on demand.

Daily Planners: Prompt: "***Make me a holiday week planner with meal prep, gift shopping, and one hour of me-time each day.***"

Stress Check-Ins: "***Give me 3 calming exercises to do before guests arrive.***"

Holiday Budget Helper: "***Create a gift budget for 6 people under $200 total.***"

The Positive Wrap-Up

At the end of the day, the holidays are fleeting. Your bot can remind you of that perspective.

Prompt: "***Help me write a note to myself that says this stress will pass, and the holiday is about connection, not perfection.***"

Or: "***Give me a motivational message I can read out loud before opening my front door to guests.***"

You Will Make It Through

The holidays can feel like they stretch forever, but they're just a season - not a sentence. With a little help from prompts, planning, and humor, you'll survive the chaos, maybe even enjoy it.

Remember: a burnt turkey is just dinner, not destiny. A late text is just a moment, not a memory. And one extra glass of wine is just tomorrow's nap waiting to happen.

You've got this. The holidays will soon be over - and you'll be proud of how you made it through.

Chapter 12. Chatting with Your Bot When You're Stressed

The holidays aren't only about food and gifts. They bring pressure, expectation, and the kind of emotional weather that can feel harder to navigate than an icy road. Stress shows up in different ways: overeating, overspending, or just lying awake at night replaying a tough conversation.

The good news? You don't have to carry all of it alone. ChatGPT can be your private sounding board, a safe space where no judgment waits, only support. Sometimes you need someone to listen, sometimes you need a practical plan, and sometimes you just need to laugh. A chatbot can do all three.

A Safe Place to Vent

When emotions run high, you may not want to burden family or friends. Chatting with your bot lets you put your feelings into words without interruption. Simply say:

- *"I need to get something off my chest. Can you just listen and reflect back what I say?"*
- *"Help me reframe this situation so I don't spiral."*

Your words can then be turned into a journal entry, a private note, or even a prayer if that helps you process.

- How to talk through stressful situations with your bot
- How to ask for calming exercises like breathing or gratitude prompts
- How to role-play a conversation before you have it with a real person
- How to write out your feelings and turn them into a journal entry or a prayer

Sample Prompts:

- ***"I am feeling overwhelmed. Can you help me break my tasks into smaller steps?"***
- ***"Give me a 5-minute guided gratitude exercise I can do right now."***
- ***"Help me practice telling my family that I cannot host the holiday dinner this year."***
- ***"Write a calming bedtime story for me to read before sleep."***

A Safe Place to Vent

When emotions run high, you may not want to burden family or friends. Chatting with your bot lets you put your feelings into words without interruption. Simply say:

- *"I need to get something off my chest. Can you just listen and reflect back what I say?"*
- *"Help me reframe this situation so I don't spiral."*

Your words can then be turned into a journal entry, a private note, or even a prayer if that helps you process.

Stress Management

Holiday stress can pile up until it feels unmanageable. ChatGPT can:

- Lead you through breathing exercises: "Guide me through a five-count inhale and exhale pattern."
- Offer quick grounding techniques: "Give me 3 sensory prompts to calm down when I feel overwhelmed."
- Create daily affirmations: *"Write me five encouraging lines I can repeat when I wake up."*

Weight and Wellness Balance

Rich foods and endless snacks can leave you feeling guilty. Instead of beating yourself up, lean on your bot to find balance:

- *"Make me a lighter menu for tomorrow to balance today's big dinner."*
- *"Remind me of three simple swaps to cut sugar without feeling deprived."*
- *"Create a quick 10-minute movement routine I can do in the living room."*

The point isn't punishment — it's creating gentle structure and reminding yourself that one day of indulgence doesn't undo your health.

Money and Holiday Spending

Overspending can be one of the most stressful parts of the season. A bot can act like a calm financial coach, helping you see what's possible without judgment.

- *"Help me set a $300 holiday gift budget and divide it between six people."*

- *"Suggest meaningful low-cost gifts that don't feel cheap."*
- *"Write me a script to decline going in on a group gift I can't afford."*

With prompts like these, you can keep your finances in control without losing the joy of giving.

Practicing Hard Conversations

Sometimes the holidays require saying "no." Role-playing with a bot helps you find the right words:

- ***"Help me practice telling my family I can't host the dinner this year."***
- ***"Write me a kind but firm message to decline an invite without guilt."***
- ***"Help me rehearse how to ask my boss for time off around the holidays."***

This practice builds confidence so the real conversation feels lighter.

Turning Feelings into Words

If you can't sleep, try giving your bot this simple task:

- ***"Write me a calming bedtime story where I am the main character and everything works out."***
- ***"Turn my worry into a gratitude list so I can see the positives."***

Expressing feelings on the page transforms them from a storm into something you can step back from and understand.

Sample Prompts Recap

- ***"I am feeling overwhelmed. Can you help me break my tasks into smaller steps?"***
- ***"Give me a 5-minute guided gratitude exercise I can do right now."***
- ***"Help me practice telling my family that I cannot host the holiday dinner this year."***
- ***"Write a calming bedtime story for me to read before sleep."***

- "Help me create a $200 holiday budget and stick to it."
- "Suggest healthier versions of my favorite holiday treats."
- "Remind me this season is temporary and will pass soon."

The Holiday Reminder

Stress, weight worries, money strain, or family pressure — none of these define the season. The holidays are not about perfection. They're about connection, memories, and making it through with your sanity intact.

Your chatbot is here to remind you of that, 24 hours a day, without judgment.

When you feel overwhelmed, just type. Let the words flow. Sometimes the best gift you can give yourself is a pause, a plan, and the reminder:

You will get through this. The season will end, the stress will pass, and you will be stronger on the other side.

Appendix: Printables & Templates

One of the best ways to ease holiday stress is to take ideas out of your head and put them down on paper. These simple templates and printables give you a place to organize, plan, and play. They're flexible, reusable, and designed to help you enjoy the season instead of worrying about it.

Holiday Planners & Calendars

Use these to block out busy days, plan meals, and set aside quiet moments.

Template Prompt:

- ***"Make me a two-week December calendar with space for meals, shopping lists, and self-care breaks."***

Sample Layout:

Date	To-Dos	Meals	Notes
Dec 10	Shop for wrapping paper	Chili	Evening: quiet time
Dec 11	Office party	Leftovers	Remember white-elephant gift

Recipe Cards

Keep your favorite recipes together and share them with family. A few blank lines are all you need.

Sample Layout:

Recipe Title:
Ingredients:
Directions:
Notes/Variations:

Prompt to Use:

- **"Turn my text recipe into a recipe card format with ingredients in a checklist."**

Craft Templates

Homemade touches bring charm to the holidays. Use simple outlines for ornaments, tags, or paper garlands.
Ideas to Include:

- Snowflake cut-outs
- Gift tag templates
- Ornament coloring shapes

Prompt to Use:

- "**Give me three holiday craft templates I can print and cut out for kids**."

Holiday Ad Copy Swipe File

Whether you're writing a family newsletter, a social media post, or a small-business holiday ad, having pre-written copy saves time.

Examples:

- *Warm & Personal:* "Wishing you a season of light, laughter, and the little things that matter most."

- *Sales Friendly:* "Still searching for the perfect gift? Our doors are open, our shelves are full, and your holiday magic is waiting."
- *Last-Minute Push:* "Don't stress — there's still time to give a thoughtful gift. Order today and we'll take care of the rest."

Prompt to Use:

- "***Write me five short holiday ad copy lines for Instagram posts with a cheerful, stress-free tone***."

How to Use This Appendix

You can copy these directly into your journal, print them out, or ask your chatbot to expand them into fresh versions that fit your exact needs. The point isn't to be perfect — it's to create a structure that helps you breathe easier.

A Final Word: Give Yourself Permission

Holidays don't have to be a test of endurance. They're just days on the calendar - and you have more freedom than you think. You're allowed to shape the season to fit your life, not the other way around.

Slow down. Step outside. Drive through a neighborhood glowing with lights. Roll down your windows and let the music spill out into the cold air. Sip a hot chocolate in your car or at a café.

Wander through a shopping center simply to admire the decorations without buying a thing. Sit at a bar and watch strangers enjoy themselves. These little moments bring you back to yourself, remind you that the world is still bigger than your to-do list.

If Christmas feels too heavy, move it. Celebrate on the 26th or the 27th or whenever you're ready.

Adjust the plan to your calendar instead of letting someone else's expectations run the show. Keep it easy, keep it simple.

When January 1 arrives, the rush will already be fading into a blur, but you'll still have your small, beautiful memories - the ones you actually enjoyed.

And remember you're an adult. You can excuse yourself from people or situations that drain you. You don't have to step on anyone's toes or make grand declarations. A polite "*I have something else to do*" is often enough. Boundaries are a gift you give yourself.

Most of all, don't let the season steal your peace. Do what feels good. Create your own rhythm. Use your chatbot as a friend, a planner, a guide, or just a safe place to vent. It can't cancel Christmas, but it can help you get through it with more grace, humor, and heart.

Give yourself permission to enjoy

the season on your own terms.

That's the best gift of all.

Just like in life, good manners matter. I always tell my ChatGPT bot "thank you."

At the end of a long day, when I've asked it to work hard and help me through so many tasks, I close with gratitude: *"Thank you for the great day."*

It may be just a tool, but treating it with kindness keeps me grounded and reminds me to practice gratitude in every part of my life.

Thank You

A Letter from the Author

Dear Reader,

Thank you for taking the time to read my book. My hope is simple: that you feel lighter and freer this holiday season. Slow down. Sip hot chocolate. Drive past glowing lights with the windows cracked and your favorite music playing. Celebrate on the day that works for you, not the day that pressures you.

Protect your peace and choose joy.

When stress creeps in, remember you're not alone. You have tools - and even a friendly chatbot - to help you plan, vent, budget, and breathe. Use it to rehearse conversations, make meal plans, or just get a pep talk. Let it be your quiet companion.

Here's to holidays shaped by you, filled with small beautiful memories that linger long after the season ends.

Warmly,

Sugar Gay Isber McMillan

About the Author

Sugar Gay Isber McMillan is a full-time writer, artist, and creative force with a degree in journalism and a lifelong love of storytelling. She has built a career as a technical writer for a global technology company, where she specializes in making complex ideas simple, clear and human.

Outside her professional work, Sugar has published more than fifty books across multiple genres. Her catalog includes:

- **Adult coloring books** that double as art history lessons, introducing readers to treasures from the Renaissance, Japanese design masters, stained glass innovators, and more - all through the relaxing medium of coloring. Available in Spanish, French and Japanese, too.
- **Books about AI and chatbots**, showing readers how to use digital tools for creativity, problem-solving, and everyday life. Talk to Your Tools series.
- **Memoirs and guided journals**, designed to help people capture and share their own life stories.

- **Novels and imaginative tales**, including poetic storybooks and speculative fiction.

No matter the genre, her work carries a consistent theme: making life more creative, more beautiful, and more manageable.

Sugar has also been recognized as a jewelry designer and artist, with features in exhibitions, magazines, and teaching roles at Austin Community College. But her passion now centers on writing - using words to connect, inspire, and empower.

To explore more of Sugar's books, visit her growing catalog online or connect with her directly:

- **Instagram:** @SugarGayIsber
- **Amazon Author Page:** search *Sugar Gay Isber McMillan*
- **Hashtags:** #SugarGayIsberBooks #ColorCreateConnect

Her readers describe her as "a writer who makes complicated things feel simple, serious things feel lighter, and ordinary things feel magical." Whether you pick up one book or fifty, you'll always find a spark of joy in her pages.

Coloring & Art History Series

- Color, Create & Connect™ with Art History
- Learn While You Color™

AI & Writing Guides

- Talk to Your Tools™

Memoir & Journaling

- Hold Your Memories Gently™

Storybooks

- Tom & The Secret Color™
- The Prompt Whisper™ (fits both AI + creative nonfiction side)

Spend an hour creating beauty,
and you'll carry calm with you all day."

Share Your Thoughts

If you enjoyed this book, please consider leaving an honest review on Amazon or Goodreads.

Your feedback helps other readers find it and supports indie authors like me in creating more.

What Early Readers Are Saying

"A warm, practical companion for surviving the holidays with less stress."

"Full of simple tips that really helped me breathe easier this season."

"Reading this felt like talking with a friend who has all the answers."

Sugar Gay Isber McMillan

@SugarGayIsber on Instagram

Sugar Gay Isber McMillan
Books on Amazon

GayIsber.com

Made in United States
North Haven, CT
05 November 2026

21767253R00063